MW00983330

HEART OF LOVE

Saint Thérèse of Lisieux

VERITAS

Published 1998 by
Veritas Publications
7-8 Lower Abbey Street
Dublin 1

Reprinted 2000, 2001

ISBN 1 85390 398 1

The material reproduced in this publication was first published by the Carmelite Commission of Ireland in 1996/7, to celebrate the centenary of the death of St Thérèse of Lisieux, 30 September 1997. The final chapter, 'Doctor of the Church', was first published in the July/August 1997 edition of *Spirituality* and is reprinted with the kind permission of Dominican Publications.

Cover illustration: icon of St Thérèse by Sr Paula OCSO, in the Carmelite Retreat Centre, Avila, Dublin.
Cover design by Barbara Croatto
Printed in the Republic of Ireland by Betaprint Ltd, Dublin

Contents

Introduction

30 September 1997 marked the centenary of the death of St Thérèse of Lisieux. A huge explosion of interest occurred in every part of the Christian world – with international seminars, lectures, new critical studies, a profusion of popular books and articles and an unexpected amount of media interest and coverage. A hundred years after her death Thérèse is still the best known and the best loved of modern saints.

Few saints have had such a profound influence on the spirituality of the twentieth century. Her message is as simple as it is profound. It speaks with gospel clarity and directness to a world weary with its own confusion and complexity. It is a message of hope within despair, of faith within uncertainty; it is the proclamation of the triumph of love as the only ultimate answer to the restless searching of the human heart. Love is at the heart of Thérèse's life and message. 'Sometimes I seek for another word to express love', she wrote to her cousin Marie Guérin, 'but on this earth words are powerless to express all the soul's vibrations, so we have to keep to this one word: love'. For her love never lost its meaning or its power to transform every moment into grace.

The pages that follow are an attempt to capture something of the beauty and simplicity of the message of Thérèse of Lisieux. They were originally written as separate leaflets, easy to read and carry, and presented as part of the general literature of the centenary year. They cover the story of her soul and of the book in which it is recorded and they draw together the main elements of her Little Way – prayer, gospel simplicity, hope, mercy and trust. There are ample quotations from Thérèse's own writings, especially from her recently translated poems and a wide selection of her own prayers as well as prayers to her.

The crowning glory of the centenary year was the declaration of Thérèse as Doctor of the Church. Once and for all it has highlighted her universal mission and world-wide appeal. As never before she now belongs to the whole Church and her message vibrates with renewed clarity and urgency. The Little Flower, once nicknamed 'the little doctor', has become the great doctor, the doctor of the Little Way of trust and confidence. She stands with 'the giants of faith', her words and her teaching proclaiming, for a new century and a new millennium, the eternal message of love, mercy and forgiveness. Love is the very core of the Gospel message; it is also at the very heart of the message of Thérèse of Lisieux.

Had the learned who spent their lives in study come to me, undoubtedly they would have been astonished to see a child of fourteen understand perfection's secrets, secrets all their knowledge cannot reveal because to possess them one has to be poor in spirit!

The Genius of St Thérèse

The Church has always had its saints and always will. New names are continually added to the calendar. Already during the pontificate of Pope John Paul II, over one hundred new saints have been raised to the altar.

A saint is a gift from God to the Church and, indeed, for that matter, to the world. Every saint is a masterpiece of grace, someone that the faithful may imitate and through whom they offer their prayers to God.

But a saint is also a product of his or her own time. Often their lives are prophetic and their message of particular relevance to the men and women of their own age.

> *'I always wanted to be a great saint, even though I was only too aware of my own weakness and poverty.'*

St Thérèse of Lisieux was no exception. No other saint has exerted such an enormous influence on the twentieth century. Though her life was short, hidden and, for the most part, without social or political dimension, she was fully in tune with the spirit of her age. She asked the same questions, wrestled with the same problems and faced the same pain and anguish as many of her contemporaries.

Who were her contemporaries – the great names that dominated the thought and development of the twentieth century? During her life the writings of Karl Marx were already influencing the pattern of social and economic thought; Sigmund Freud had published his first explorations into psychoanalysis; Charles Darwin's theories of evolution were challenging the way people thought about themselves and a new school of existential philosophy was profoundly affecting the culture and literature of the age.

Thérèse herself may never have heard of any of these names, and she certainly never read any of their writings. Yet, in her own way and in her own world – the world of the spirit – she was as creative and as adventurous in her thinking as any of them. She too confronted the loneliness and despair that was to characterise the present century. Her world may have been small but it was not narrow. She herself prayed that her heart would always be as large and spacious as the towering Alps she had seen on her trip to Rome. And, indeed, so it was. Thérèse did not pull back from the abyss, she did not evade the issues. Her faith and her love did not shield her from the pain and anguish that confronts every genuine seeker after truth. She sought no easy path to sanctity. She experienced within herself the eternal struggle of the human heart to purify itself of selfishness and smallness and open itself to love. She knew the struggle between darkness and faith, between despair and hope and between the real and the counterfeit.

'Lord, what is the truth? Let me see things as they are, let me never be deceived.'

Thérèse was not afraid of living the truth, no matter what the consequences. Few people could say with the same conviction as she did a few hours before she died 'I have never sought anything but the truth.' Living the truth was not easy for her, surrounded as she was, for the most part, by the sentimental, the pious and the unreal.

But, on her own, like an explorer, she persevered. And through the sheer force of her love and her burning desire to know the true heart of God, she discovered, for herself and for others, the forgotten truths of Christianity. Without realising it she was giving back to the Church and to the world the God of the Gospel.

The greatness of St Thérèse was not that she experienced these truths, or even that she wrote about them, but that she lived them at white heat. She did not move in a world of theory or arid speculation. Her concern was with life and with finding the secret of transforming life with meaning. This she did and in doing so became a source of light and warmth for others as well.

> *'Because I was little and weak He lowered Himself to me, and instructed me secretly in the things of His love.'*

Every saint reflects the Gospel in one way or another. But not every saint is a reformer or an innovator and not every saint is a spiritual genius. St Thérèse was such and can rightly take her place among the handful of truly great men and women who have changed the history of spirituality – Paul, Augustine, Francis of Assisi, her namesake Teresa of Avila, Vincent de Paul, John Bosco. She can be counted among those revolutionary beings who have drawn new and creative insights from the eternal treasury of the Gospel.

Every reformer is at heart a simplifier just as Jesus was. And every reform contains within itself the seed of revolution. Thérèse started a revolution of infinite consequences, since it is based on the Gospel itself.

> *'Oh! How sweet is the way of love! How I want to apply myself to doing the will of God always with the greatest self-surrender.'*

Her influence is great because she expressed herself simply and in a way everyone can understand. Her concepts are universal – trust, surrender, love, mercy – but she revitalised them and gave them back their original beauty. Everything about her is full of life and conviction and she impressed her own creative genius on a fresh and original expression of the Christian message. Since the early days of

Christianity no one has provided a more direct and inspired shortcut to the Gospel.

She was one of the first to break the rigid and narrow mould of conservatism that had characterised the nineteenth century and that only finally erupted in Vatican II. She helped us to return to the Scriptures, deepened our awareness of being part of the Church, healed us of Jansenism and showed us once again the human face of God. She unmasked fear and proclaimed the triumph of love.

Thérèse of Lisieux touched the core of the human spirit, where the whole fragile world of men and women meets. She found strength in weakness, victory in defeat, life in death. She released the human spirit and set holiness free.

FROM HER WRITINGS

Why do I desire to communicate the secrets of your love, O Jesus, for was it not you alone who taught them to me, and can you not reveal them to others as well? Yes, I know you can and I beg you to do so.

I find myself at a period of my life when I can cast a glance upon the past; my soul has matured in the crucible of exterior and interior sufferings. And now, like a flower strengthened by the storm, I can raise my head and see the words of Psalm 22 realised in me: 'The Lord is my Shepherd, I shall not want.'

Even though I had on my conscience all the sins that can be committed, I would go, my heart broken with sorrow, and throw myself into the arms of Jesus, for I know how much he loves the prodigal child who returns to him.

My Song for Today

My life is but an instant
a passing hour.
My life is but a day that escapes
and flies away.
My God, you know that
to love you here on earth
I only have today!

Poem no. 5

Prayer of petition

Father in heaven, we thank you
for the life and teaching
of St Thérèse of the Child Jesus.
Through her you remind us
of your infinite love
and of your fatherly care
for all your children.
You filled her with
the spirit of love
and gave her the grace
to make you known and loved.
Help us also to love you
and to make you greatly loved.

Story of a Soul

When she died in 1897, St Thérèse of the Child Jesus and of the Holy Face – the Little Flower – was unknown outside of her own convent and a small circle of family and friends. Twenty-seven years later almost half a million people gathered in Rome for her canonisation.

She has been called 'the greatest saint of modern times' and, one hundred years after her death, her life is still an inspiration and a challenge. Lisieux has become a household name, and her Little Way an accepted part of Christian spirituality.

How can we explain the 'storm of glory' that has made her the best loved of modern saints? What is her message and the charm of her appeal?

The popular image of St Thérèse, found in so many churches and repositories around the world, gives a rather stylised image of the saint, complete with a large crucifix, rose petals and angelic smile.

> *I did not have either a guide or a light except that which burned in my heart.*

Thérèse was a strong woman, full of courage and determination. She was not born a saint. She struggled with her own difficult temperament. She experienced failure and disappointment and only came to know the power of God's grace through accepting her own weakness and limitation.

Thérèse Martin was born in Alençon in France on 2 January 1873. She was the last of nine children, four of whom had already died. Her father was a watchmaker and her mother ran a small lace-making business. When Thérèse was four her mother died and the family moved to Lisieux. Here she spent the next ten years of her life, brought up in an atmosphere of love and affection.

From an early age, she wanted to give herself totally to God. She struggled with her own stubbornness of will and suffered a lot because of her very sensitive and scrupulous nature. When she was ten years old, she was cured of a mysterious illness through the ' smile of the Queen of Heaven'.

> *The Good Lord gave me a father and a mother more worthy of heaven than earth.*

At the age of fifteen, she entered the Carmelite Convent in Lisieux and was given the name 'Thérèse of the Child Jesus'. She spent the next nine years of her life there, faithfully and heroically living the life of a Carmelite nun with great simplicity and humility. She discovered what she called her 'Little Way' – a way of confidence and trust and of total surrender to God's Merciful Love. At the end of her life she realised that her mission was about to begin and she would spend her heaven doing good upon earth.

> *God was able in a very short time to draw me out from the narrow circle in which I was turning without knowing how to come out.*

Before she died, Thérèse, under obedience, began writing down the recollections and memories of her childhood together with her reflections on the religious life.

St Thérèse died on 30 September 1897 at the age of twenty-four. She was canonised in 1925. She has been proclaimed a Patroness of France and the Missions. Her autobiography, *Story of a Soul*, was published one year after her death. Millions of copies have been sold and it has been translated into over fifty languages.

Such, in broad outline, is the life of St Thérèse of Lisieux. But behind the facts and the dates, lies the deeper story – the story of a human being, a saint of God, who made the greatest journey towards sanctity and the fullness of Christian life.

> *My first recollections are of loving smiles and tender caresses: but if God made others love me so much, He made me love them too, for I was of an affectionate nature.*

> *Blessed are you, Lord, for hiding these things from the wise and clever and revealing them to little children.*
> Lk 10:21

FROM HER WRITINGS

My Joy!

Happiness – people search for it
In vain: it's not on earthly ground:
With me, it's quite the opposite –
It's in my heart that joy is found.
This joy – don't think it comes and goes:
Coming to me, it came to stay.
Delighting like a fresh spring rose
It smiles upon me every day.

Poem no. 45. Translated by Alan Bancroft

God made me understand that
my glory would not be seen by human eyes,
but that it would consist in
becoming a great saint.
This desire can appear daring
when I consider how weak
and imperfect I am.
But I have the bold confidence
that I can be a saint,
if I do not rely on myself.
Rather, I trust in Him
who will raise me to Himself.

We naturally think of someone we love.
I doubt if I have ever been
three minutes without thinking of Him.

I have never given God anything but love.
Love is the only thing that matters.
No, I did not fight hard.
I loved, loved deeply.

Prayer to St Thérèse of the Child Jesus

O little Thérèse of the Child Jesus.
During your short life on earth,
you became a shining example
of Christian virtue.
Of love, strong as death
and of whole-hearted
abandonment to God.
Teach me your Little Way
of trust and surrender.
Fill my heart with a true love
for God and for others.
Make me a child of God,
our loving Father,
so that, like you,
I may walk the road of confidence
and love.

Saints never grow old.
They never become figures of the past,
men and women of 'yesterday'.
On the contrary, they are always
men and women of the future,
witnesses of the world to come.

Pope John Paul II – Lisieux, 1980

The Story of a Book

'It seems to me, that if a little flower could speak, it would simply tell what God had done for it without trying to hide its blessings.

The flower about to tell her story rejoices at having to publish the totally free gifts God has given to her.

She knows that nothing in herself was capable of attracting the Divine favours, and His mercy alone brought about everything that is good.'

The Christian world first came to know of St Thérèse of Lisieux through her autobiography, published just one year to the day after her death. The publication was the spark that set off a conflagration. Within months it was reprinted and has never been out of circulation since. Today, it is in its ninetieth French edition and has been translated into over fifty languages. Few books have had a more profound influence on the spirituality of the twentieth century.

> *Before taking my pen, I knelt before the statue*
> *of Mary and begged her to guide my hand*
> *so that it wrote nothing displeasing to her.*

Yet the fact remains that St Thérèse of Lisieux never 'wrote a book' as such. What was published in 1898 as the *Story of a Soul* was in fact three different manuscripts, written for three different persons.

The first manuscript, written in 1895, is addressed to her older sister Pauline, Mother Agnes, who was Prioress at the time. It was meant simply as a 'family souvenir' for her own sisters and contains childhood memories and recollections together with some of her experiences during her first years in the convent.

The second, only three pages of folded paper in very small handwriting, was written the following year for her eldest sister Marie. There is every indication that it was written in great haste and in a state of extreme fatigue. But it is the jewel of all her writings, for in it she reveals the secret of her Little Way and tells of her discovery of her vocation to be love in the heart of the Church.

The final manuscript is addressed to the new Prioress, Mother Marie de Gonzague. It was written just a few months before Thérèse died, much of it in her invalid chair under the chestnut trees. Thérèse was already in a state of extreme exhaustion, and had to finish her writing in pencil, so great was her weakness.

The *Story of a Soul*, published in 1898, was in fact a compilation of all three manuscripts, edited by her sister Pauline. Even though it was a faithful presentation of the central doctrine of St Thérèse, in time the demand grew for the publication of the manuscripts in full, exactly as Thérèse had written them. This was finally done in 1957 with the photostat publication of the three original manuscripts.

Childhood memories written on a penny copybook, a farewell note to an older sister and the random thoughts of a dying nun, have all come together to produce one of the greatest spiritual classics of our age. For behind the scribbled notes we find a humble, joyful acknowledgement of the mercy and goodness of God, written in a fresh, vivid style. A childlike simplicity and a delightful sense of humour shine through every line. But, above all, we see a young woman totally possessed by God, who poured out her life in unselfish love, ardent prayer and complete surrender.

I feel that my mission is soon to begin,
to make others love God as I do,
to teach others my 'Little Way'.
I will spend my Heaven doing good upon earth.

I am going to stammer some words even though
I feel it is quite impossible for the human tongue
to express things which the human heart
can hardly understand.

Writings of St Thérèse of the Child Jesus

Autobiography: *The Story of a Soul*
Letters: 266 in all, written mostly to her own sisters in the convent, members of the family circle and her missionary 'brothers'.
Poems: 54, written for feastdays or special occasions.
Plays: Thérèse wrote 8 plays for community recreation.
Prayers: 21 in all, including her Act of Offering to Merciful Love.
Last Conversations: a record of her conversations with her sisters during the last six months of her life.

FROM HER WRITINGS

Dearest Mother, it is to you that I am going to confide the story of my soul. When you first asked me to do so I was frightened. But since then Our Lord has made it clear to me that all He wants is plain obedience. In any case, what I shall be doing is only what will be my task for all eternity – telling over and over again the story of God's mercies to me.

To her sister Pauline

How will this 'Story of a Little Flower' come to an end? Perhaps the little flower will be plucked in her youthful freshness or else transplanted to other shores. I don't know, but what I am certain about is that God's mercy will accompany her always.

After my death you must speak to no one about my manuscript before it is published, the devil will lay more than one trap to hinder God's work, a very important work.

To her sister Pauline

The heart of a child does not seek after riches and glory. What this child asks for is love. In fact she knows only one thing – to love God with all her heart. Great works may be forbidden her, she cannot preach the Gospel or shed her blood. All she can do is sing for ever the canticle of love.

At the Close of my Life

Divine Saviour, at the close of my life
Come and search for me without a shadow of delay.
Show me your infinite tenderness
And the sweetness of your glance.
With what love your voice calls to me
Saying to me – all is pardoned.
Come to my heart,
which you have loved so much.

Poem no. 41

Prayer to St Thérèse of the Child Jesus

Teach us to open our hearts
without reserve
to the Holy Spirit
as you did,
to seek and find God's will
in all the crises and choices,
in the joys and disappointments
of our lives.
Gain for us too
the grace to do His will
with courage and untroubled hearts
so that we may radiate a joy and a
gladness like yours
in the service of Our Lord.

St Thérèse and Prayer

For me, prayer is an aspiration of the heart,
it is a simple glance directed to heaven,
it is a cry of gratitude and love in the midst of
trial as well as joy.
Finally, it is something great and
supernatural, which expands my soul
and unites me to Jesus.

How great is the power of prayer!
It could be called a queen,
who has free access
at every moment to the King
and who can always
obtain what she asks.

One of the delightful incidents which St Thérèse recalls from her early childhood is the day one of the teachers at the Abbey school asked her how she spent her holidays. To her surprise, Thérèse said she spent a lot of her time 'hidden behind the bed thinking; thinking about God, about life and about eternity'. 'I now see,' Thérèse reflects, 'that I was praying without realising it.'

My thoughts went very deep at such times and, although
I knew nothing about meditation, my soul did sink into
a genuine state of prayer.

Thérèse did not talk or write a lot about prayer. Yet her whole life was one of prayer. 'I came to the convent,' she said, 'to save souls and especially to pray for priests.' Prayer is an essential ingredient of the Little Way; the atmosphere of spiritual childhood. She herself had no doubt about its power or its necessity. 'What would I do without prayer?' she asks. 'It is one of the all-powerful weapons God has put into my hands'.

Prayer, for St Thérèse, in its simplest expression, was nothing else but a thought turned Godwards: 'a launching out towards God, an opening of the heart, a binding of the soul more closely to Him'.

> *Outside of the Prayer of the Church, which I am unworthy to recite, I do not have the courage to search out beautiful prayers in books. There are so many of them and it really gives me a headache and besides each prayer is more beautiful that the other.*

In a significant incident in her own life, she discovered the practical value of prayer. A notorious criminal, Pranzini, was condemned to die. Thérèse prayed earnestly and fervently for him and her prayer was answered. Just before he died, Pranzini took the crucifix offered to him and kissed it. It was all Thérèse wanted. She had received her sign. Prayer could work miracles.

For her it was all very logical. After all, if God was her father then it was only natural for her to turn to Him with childlike trust and confidence. She did not have to worry about saying the right words. It was the attitude of the heart that mattered. 'Complicated prayers are all very well', she said, 'but they are not for simple souls'. She was not able to use the splendid formulas given in books, so, 'I simply do what children do before they learn to read.' She poured out her thoughts and feelings in her own way and God never failed to understand. 'He never gets tired of listening to the tales of my joys and griefs – as if He hadn't heard them all before!'

I could not take my eyes off the sea: its vastness, the ceaseless roaring of its waves, spoke to me of the greatness and power of God.

Children may not express their ideas very well but they can always communicate in their own way. For Thérèse prayer was essentially communication; sometimes in words, at other times simply by a look, a sigh or a tear. Often it was in silence and frequently in darkness and weariness: 'What excuse have I, after so many years in the convent, for falling asleep at prayer?' But she never gave in to discouragement. She used the image of Jesus 'asleep in the boat'; she was happy to know He was there and to let Him rest: 'I assure you He does not have to keep up a conversation with me!'

For Thérèse, prayer was like a magnet drawing down God's grace upon the world. It was not just Pranzini, but a whole world that she could reach out to and help by her prayers. 'This is what my prayer is like,' she wrote. 'I ask Our Lord to draw me into the furnace of His love, so that its effects can be felt by all those that I love.' Her life was a prayer and her prayer was love. Perhaps her deathbed conversation with her sister Celine is the best illustration of this.

'What are you doing? You ought to try to sleep.'
'I cannot. I am praying.'
'What are you saying to Jesus?'
'I say nothing... I just love Him.'

FROM HER WRITINGS

It is much better to talk to God
than to talk about him.

Was it not in prayer that the saints and so many other famous friends of God found the secret of their wisdom?

A scholar has said: 'Give me a lever and a fulcrum and I will lift the world'. Archimedes was not talking to God, so this request was not granted. But the saints really have obtained this privilege in all its fullness.

The fulcrum God told them to use was himself, nothing less than himself, and the lever was prayer.

Only it must be the kind of prayer that sets the heart on fire with love.

This is how the saints in our day have lifted up the world, and that is how they will continue to do so till the end of time.

Really I should be very upset for having slept so many times during my hours of prayer and thanksgiving after Communion; but I am not.

I remember that children are as pleasing to their parents when they are asleep as well as when they are awake.

Prayer of a Child

Remember thou
that erstwhile here below
to care for us
was thy sole happiness.
O hear thy children praying
and bestow thy fond protection;
deign each one to bless.
Thou foundest in the Heavens
our mother loved at rest;
She had been long already
in country of the blest.
As in that sacred land
you both together stand
watch o'er us now.

Poem no.8 (to her father). Translated by Santa Clara

Prayer to St Thérèse of the Child Jesus

O Little Thérèse of the Child Jesus
you promised to spend your heaven
doing good upon earth.
Listen attentively to my prayer
and look favourably on my request.

Speak a word for me to Mary, our Mother,
who smiled on you at the dawn of life.
I ask you, Little Flower of Jesus,
to obtain for me every blessing I need,
to strengthen me during life,
defend me at the hour of death,
and lead me to the joy and peace
of my eternal home.

At the Heart of the Gospels

'Of St Thérèse of Lisieux,
it can be said with conviction
that the Spirit of God let her reveal directly,
to the men and women of our time,
the fundamental mystery,
the reality of the Gospel:
the fact that we have really received a
"spirit of adoption which makes us cry out:
Abba Father!"
And, indeed, what truth of the Gospel
is more fundamental and
more universal than this:
God is our Father and we are his children?'

Pope John Paul II – Lisieux 1980

When St Thérèse visited Rome in 1887, one of the places she went to see was the Church and Shrine of St Cecilia. She describes the visit in her autobiography and quotes a verse of a hymn of St Cecilia which says 'the Gospel rested on her heart'. The same can be said with equal truth about Thérèse herself.

She is, above all else, the saint of the Gospels. She loved the Gospels, reading them constantly, copying and comparing texts and quoting them effortlessly. In fact her writings contain over a thousand quotations from the Scriptures. She almost knew them by heart, from her constant meditation and reflection on them. She even carried a small copy of the Gospels close to her heart night and day. Indeed, one writer said of her that it was not a saint that was canonised in May 1925 but the Gospel itself!

Your words, O Jesus, are mine and I can make use of them to draw on the souls united to me the favours of the heavenly Father.

St Thérèse did not invent her Little Way; she discovered it in the Gospels. By her own admission the Gospels became her daily food and sustained her in her time of prayer. 'I find in the Gospels everything I need. I am constantly finding in them new lights, hidden and mysterious meanings.' For her the small book of the Gospels became an unerring compass and a beacon of light along the spiritual path.

I searched the Scriptures for a sign and I read these words coming from the mouth of the Eternal Wisdom: 'whoever is little let them come to me'. I felt I had found what I was looking for.

To understand the message of St Thérèse of Lisieux is in fact to understand the Gospels. Essentially her doctrine is nothing else but a fresh and vigorous restatement of the basic Christian truths.

The heart of her discovery was that the God of Revelation was a God of love and mercy. For her the 'Good News' of the Gospel was summed up in St John's cryptic phrase 'God is Love'. The meaning of the incarnation, as she understood it, was to make this love visible.

She had a special love for the parables, the stories Jesus told of mercy, healing and forgiveness. Hence her joy at the so called 'Gospel love scenes': the woman at the well, the good thief, Mary Magdalene – where love and mercy overlap. 'I have only to cast a glance at the Gospel – immediately I breathe the perfume of Jesus and I know which way to run.'

As for me, with the exception of the Gospel, I no longer find anything in books.

The Gospels are enough. I listen with delight
to these words of Jesus which tell me all I must do:
'learn of me for I am meek and humble of heart';
then I am at peace, for according to his sweet
promise: 'you will find rest for your souls'.

Last Conversations – 15 May

Thérèse found inspiration in the pages of the Old Testament as much as in those of the Gospels. In fact, it was a simple quotation from the Book of Proverbs: 'if anyone is little, let them come to me', that launched her on her quest for spiritual childhood.

And she found confirmation of her discovery in the prophet Isaiah and the first biblical reference to God as 'mother': 'as one who a mother caresses, so will I comfort you; you will be carried at the breast and on the knee I will caress you' (Isaiah 66:13).

Thérèse refused to accept anything but the truth. She bypassed the faded images of God that were commonplace in her day and went straight to the Gospels themselves.

There she discovered the Fatherhood of God – loving, tender and forgiving. There too she discovered the hidden face of Christ, revealing, in flesh and blood, the gentle sweetness of a God who was a Saviour and a Redeemer.

One hundred years after her death, St Thérèse of Lisieux invites us to return to the Scriptures, to build our lives on the words and teaching of Jesus and to rediscover the joy of breaking the 'word of God' for ourselves and for each other.

From Her Writings

Jesus has no need of books or teachers to instruct us; He, the Teacher of teachers, instructs us without the noise of words.

Having listened to these words of Jesus there is nothing left to do but to be silent and to weep with gratitude and love.

In spite of my littleness, I would like to enlighten souls as did the Prophets and the Doctors. I feel the call to be an apostle. I would like to travel over the whole earth to preach your name. I want to preach the Gospel on all five continents, even in the most distant islands.

Never have I heard Him speak, but I feel He is within me. At each moment he is guiding and instructing me what I must say and do.

I have frequently noticed that Jesus does not want me to lay up provisions. He nourishes me at each moment with a totally new food; I find it within me without knowing how it is there. I believe it is Jesus himself hidden in the depths of my heart. He is giving me the grace of acting within me, making me think of all he desires me to do at the present moment.

Show me the secrets
hidden in the Gospel.
For in this Golden Book
Is my greatest treasure.

Poem no. 24. Translated by Santa Clara

I have never before fathomed the meaning of these words of Jesus: 'the second commandment is like the first: you shall love your neighbour as yourself'.

Jesus has spoken about this many times; you might almost say on every page of the Gospel. But at the Last Supper he makes it clearer still. When he knew his disciples were burning with a more ardent love for him, he said to them, with inexpressible tenderness, 'a new commandment I give you, that you love one another as I have loved you'.

Prayer to St Thérèse of the Child Jesus

God, our Father,
You promised your kingdom
to the little ones
and the humble of heart.
Give us the grace
to walk confidently in the way
of St Thérèse of the Child Jesus,
so that helped by her prayers,
we may see your glory
and share in your kingdom.

The Little Way

Peace is mine in littleness,
when upon the way I fall;
swift my rising, on I press,
Jesus lifts me at my call.

Then with many a sweet caress,
I to Him my love confide;
when with redoubled tenderness,
He stealeth from my side.

Poem no. 45. Translated by Santa Clara

St Thérèse was not born a saint, but she ardently desired to be one. Yet she knew her own weakness. 'When I compare myself to the saints it is like the difference between a mountain that soars into the clouds and an obscure grain of sand.' But she refused to be discouraged. Instead she looked for 'a way that is direct, very short and totally new.' That we now call the Little Way – the way of spiritual childhood.

The Little Way has been described as doing by grace what the little child does by nature. Thérèse herself would have agreed with this. Her experience within her own family circle was one of security, acceptance and love. Her relationship with her father was one of deepest tenderness and affection. He was the King, she was his 'little Queen'. It was this essential experience of love and goodness that opened for her an understanding of the Fatherhood of God. 'Our Lord has shown me,' she writes, 'the only way that leads to love – it is the way of childlike trust and self-surrender, the way of a child that sleeps, afraid of nothing, safe in its father's arms.'

One day, her sister Céline found Thérèse sewing in the workroom, her eyes filled with tears. When she enquired the cause of the tears, she was surprised by Thérèse's reply. 'I've been sitting here,' she said, 'just thinking how wonderful it is to call God Father.' Because she was a child and a saint, she had penetrated the mystery 'hidden from the wise and clever and revealed to the little ones'.

Because I was little and weak, He lowered Himself to me.

The Little Way is not an end in itself – rather it is a means that leads to the fullness of life and love. At its very centre is an acceptance of our weakness and what Thérèse called our 'poverty' – a recognition of our continuous need for God's sustaining hand. 'Tell me in a few words,' her sister asked, 'what it means to remain a child?' 'It means,' Thérèse replied, 'to acknowledge one's own nothingness, to expect everything from God and not to be upset by one's failures.' For Thérèse it was very simple – children do not take a stand on virtue, neither have they to earn their own living; as long as a child is a child, the father has to support it!

To explain the meaning of her Little Way, Thérèse used the image of the 'lift' or elevator. The image was inspired by the tender words of the prophet Isaiah – 'as one whom a mother caresses so I will comfort you... you will be carried at the breast'. The 'lift' that Thérèse discovered was the arms of Jesus that would carry her safely up 'the rough stairway of perfection'.

I wanted to find a lift that would take me up to Jesus, for I am too little to climb the rough stairway of perfection. And I found in your arms, O Jesus, the lift that will take me to Heaven.

The Little Way is not 'an escape into childhood', a running away from life, from decision-making or from responsibility. It is a way of acknowledging the fact that we cannot earn eternal life by our own efforts. Eternal life is the free gift of our Father who loves us. All we have to do is accept it with the trusting heart of a child. 'Everything is a gift,' Thérèse exclaimed, and when she said everything, she meant everything. Perhaps that is why she once described the Little Way to her sister Céline as 'the way of the good thief'.

Perhaps a charming parable from Thérèse's own life best illustrates the true meaning of the Little Way: 'One day' she relates, 'one of the novices wanted to light candles for a procession. She had no matches, only a little lamp burning in front of a shrine with a tiny glimmer left in it. Nevertheless she succeeded in lighting her candle from the charred wick and with it all the candles of the community. 'Who dares to glory in their own work?' I thought. From one faint spark such as this it would be possible to set the whole world on fire. And yet, the humble little candle would remain the first cause of it all.'

No need to grow up, but rather to remain little and become so more and more.

From Her Writings

I feel my mission is about to begin, my mission of making God loved as I love Him and teaching my way to others.

I have always remained little, having no other occupation but to gather flowers, the flowers of love and sacrifice.

To be little is not to be discouraged over one's faults, for children fall often, but they are too little to hurt themselves very much. By myself I cannot attain what I desire and yet everything in my heart tells me I cannot give up, so I must bear with myself as I am with all my imperfections.

If only everyone weak and imperfect like me felt as I do, no one would ever despair of reaching the heights of love. Jesus does not ask for great deeds, He asks only for self-surrender and for gratitude. It is gratitude that brings us the most grace.

Prayer of St Thérèse for Spiritual Childhood

Lord, give me the open heart of a child.
Let me come trustingly to you,
not afraid to ask for your love.
Deliver me from the belief
that I am self-sufficient.
Show me my need of you.
Give me the grace to reach out to you.
Lord, give me a child's simplicity
and a sense of wonder.
may my enthusiasm for you never dim.
Let me hasten to converse with you
in the intimacy of prayer.
Give me discernment to realise
there is no detail of my life
too tiny for your concern.
Help me to perceive your glory
in the helplessness of the cross.
Son of God, who for my sake,
took on the dependency of childhood,
help me to accept the readiness
of the Father's grace.

Merciful Love

O Heart of Jesus,
treasured tenderness,
Thou art my joy supreme,
my hope, my all;
Thou who didst charm my youth
and sweetly bless,
Stay with me
till the twilight shadows fall.
Master, to Thee alone
my life I give,
My every longing sigh
to Thee is known;
Lost in Thy goodness infinite,
I live, O Heart of Jesus,
lost with thee alone!

Poem no. 23 to the Sacred Heart
Translated by Santa Clara

When St Thérèse's sister, Mother Agnes, was asked at the process of canonisation why she wished to see her sister canonised, she replied spontaneously: 'Because it will be for the glory of God, especially by proclaiming his mercy'. Thérèse herself would wish for nothing else. She begins her life story by saying 'I am only going to do one thing: sing the Mercies of the Lord'. And she closed the first part of her autobiography with the words 'How this story will end I do not know, but what I am certain of is that God's Mercy will accompany it forever.'

It was only when Thérèse discovered her own weakness

and poverty that she also discovered the mystery of God's mercy. And it was in the Gospels that she made her discovery. At the heart of the Christian message is the revelation that the God that Jesus came to proclaim is a God of mercy and love.

Thérèse loved to reflect and meditate on the words of Isaiah – 'ours were the sufferings he bore, ours the sorrows he carried'. She saw in the face of Christ one who entered into our world of pain and suffering so that he would identify with all our weakness and all our frailty.

> *His mercy alone has brought about everything that is good in me.*

In Him she saw a God of infinite tenderness, one who washed away the past for the woman who had been a notorious sinner, for Zacchaeus, for the woman of Samaria and for the good thief. In St Thérèse's day much of the emphasis in religious books and spirituality was on the justice of God – a God who kept account of all our faults and failings, a rigorous and unyielding God, who needed to be appeased by sacrifices and good works. Thérèse did not see it that way: 'What a sweet joy it is to think that God is just – that he takes into account our weakness, that he is perfectly aware of our fragile nature. Why should I fear then? Must not the infinitely just God who pardons the faults of the prodigal son, be just, also, to me?'

> *My way is all trust and love. I don't understand those who fear so tender a Friend.*

On Sunday, 9 June 1895, the Feast of the Holy Trinity, Thérèse received a special grace 'to understand more than ever how much God wished to be loved'. She knew about those saints who had offered themselves as victims to divine justice, but she adds, 'I was far from feeling attracted to making it'. Why not, she thought, make the same offering to the divine mercy? 'After all', she reflected. 'does God's Merciful Love not need victims too?' She would open her heart like a vessel, to receive 'the waves of infinite tenderness' that he wished to pour out on the world.

Her Act of Offering to God's Merciful Love was in itself a climax and a breakthrough in her understanding of her own spiritual journey. It was a natural development of her Little Way – another expression of the same reality, this time, in prayer form. It is the Little Way in prayer. Her offering covered every aspect of her life and spirituality. It was more than an offering, it was a total surrender to love, a great leap of trust and confidence. 'What pleases God most', she told her sister Marie, 'is the blind trust I have in His mercy. This is my only treasure.'

In the copy of the Gospels that she always carried with her, Thérèse had written on a picture card two sentences from the Gospel. On one side the words of Peter: 'Lord, you know that I love you', and on the other, the words of the publican: 'Lord, be merciful to me, a sinner'. It would be hard to sum up more accurately the spirituality of St Thérèse of Lisieux and her understanding of the God she knew and experienced as Merciful Love.

> *How little known is the great and merciful love of the Heart of Jesus. The fact is that to enjoy this treasure we must be humble and recognise our nothingness, and that is just what many people will not do.*

FROM HER WRITINGS

To me God has granted his infinite Mercy and through it I contemplate all the other divine perfections.

It is confidence and nothing but confidence that will lead us to love.

How great is His Mercy; I shall be able to sing of it only in Heaven.

We cannot have too much confidence in the good God – he is so mighty and so merciful.

Dear Jesus, how I wish I could explain to those who are conscious of their own littleness, how great your condescension is! I am certain that if you could find a soul more feeble and insignificant than mine, you would overwhelm it with graces still more extraordinary, provided that it would give itself up in entire confidence to your Infinite Mercy.

Act of Offering to Merciful Love

O my God! O Blessed Trinity,
I offer myself to Your Merciful Love
as a victim of holocaust,
so that my life may be
an act of perfect love.

Continue to consume me, Lord,
allowing the waves of infinite
tenderness pent up within you
to overflow into my soul, that I may
become a martyr of your love.

May this martyrdom prepare me
to appear before you,
causing me to die and take flight
without delay into the eternal
embrace of your Merciful Love.

I want, O My Beloved,
to renew this offering again and again,
with every beat of my heart,
until the shadows disappear
and I can tell you again of
my love, forever, face to face.

More Mother than Queen

O Sweetest star of Heaven
O virgin spotless blest.
Shining with Jesus' light,
Guiding to Him my way.
Mother, beneath thy veil,
Let my tired spirit rest.
For this brief passing day.

Poem no. 5: My Song for Today
Translated by L.S.Emery

Shortly before she died St Thérèse said to her sister Marie 'I would love to have been a priest in order to preach about the Blessed Virgin! One sermon would have been sufficient to say everything about the subject.' Thérèse never preached that sermon but she has left abundant testimony in her writings to the special place the Blessed Virgin held in her life. The last poem she wrote, 'Why I love you, O Mary', is a beautiful reflection on the life of Our Blessed Lady and a tender expression of Thérèse's intimate and childlike relationship with her.

As with everything about St Thérèse, there is an originality and a freshness in her understanding of the Blessed Virgin, so different from the sugary and exaggerated presentation of her own day. 'For a sermon on the Blessed Virgin to bear fruit', she said, 'it must show her real life, such as the Gospel has set it before us, and not some imaginary life. After all, her real life in Nazareth and afterwards must have been ordinary.'

It is in the Gospels alone that Thérèse finds the real Mary

– a woman and a mother who experienced joy and sorrow, hope and disappointment, and lived out her life in faith and love.

> *The Blessed Virgin is my dearest mother, and usually children resemble their mother.*

For Thérèse, two things mattered most in her understanding of Mary: love and imitation. 'It is all very well to speak of her virtues and prerogatives', she said, 'but we must not stop there. We must make her loved. If a sermon on Our Lady forces us from beginning to end to gasp with amazement, we soon have enough of it, and it will lead neither to love or imitation.' Thérèse never portrayed Mary as someone beyond our reach but rather as one who, in her own words 'walked the common way, experiencing cold, heat and exhaustion and who knows what suffering means'.

> *The Blessed Virgin prefers imitation to admiration as her own life was so simple.*

St Thérèse's approach to our Blessed Lady is characterised by its simplicity and sincerity. She knew that her miraculous cure at the age of ten had been the result of a special grace of the 'Virgin of the Smile'. For Thérèse, Mary is the compassionate mother who knows how to look after all her needs and take care of her requests. 'To ask something of the Blessed Virgin is not the same as to ask something of God. She knows well what to do with all my little desires and it is for her to decide whether to ask for them or not'.

Thérèse takes issue with those who say that the glory of the Blessed Virgin will eclipse that of all the saints. 'How strange that would be', she exclaims, 'a mother extinguishing the glory of her children! I believe quite the opposite, that she increases many times the glory of the elect. We all know', she reflects, 'that the Blessed Virgin is Queen of

Heaven and earth', but she adds emphatically, 'she is more Mother than Queen.'

Thérèse sees Our Lady as a model and inspiration for all who follow the Little Way. 'The number of little souls upon the earth is great', she says, 'and they can, without fear, raise their eyes to Mary'. For Thérèse, the Little Way is also Mary's way, a way of love, confidence and trust, without great deeds or outward show, reflected in the hidden life of Nazareth.

Thérèse rejoiced in the simple fact of Mary's existence. 'Who could have invented her', she asks, 'if God had not created her just as she is?' In fact, she says, 'we are much happier that she is, for she has no Blessed Virgin to love! How much more is that a joy for us and how much less it is one for her.' The last words she ever wrote, on the back of a picture of Our Lady of Victories, capture, in a special way, the tenderness of her devotion: 'Oh, Mary, if I were the Queen of Heaven and you were Thérèse, I would like to be Thérèse in order to see you Queen of heaven'.

> *I like to hide my suffering from God; but I hide nothing from the Blessed Virgin. I tell her everything.*

From Her Writings

In looking at the Blessed Virgin last night I realised that it cannot be true that she never experienced any physical suffering. I understood that she suffered not only in soul but also in body. Yes, she knew well what it is to suffer.

Yes, I am suffering very much but it is to the Blessed Virgin that I make my complaint.

Do not be afraid that you can love the Blessed Virgin too much; you will never love her enough, and Jesus will be quite pleased since she is His Mother too.

The greatest masterpiece of the heart of our God, is the heart of a mother.

Why I love you, O Mary

In pondering thy life,
as from the Gospel shown,
I dare to look upon thee.
I am in truth thy child,
to me 'tis clearly shown,
for I behold thee human
and suffering like me.

Poem no. 54. Translated by Santa Clara

St Thérèse's Act of Consecration to Our Lady

O Mary, conceived without sin,
wishing to place myself
under your special protection,
I choose you this day
as my patroness, my advocate
and my mother.
I will try with all my heart
to work for your glory
and to make you better known
and better loved.

I promise to give myself
wholeheartedly to your service,
to walk in your footsteps
and to imitate your virtues.

Obtain for me, O tender Mother,
the grace to be faithful to you
all my life,
so that I may merit the grace
of being your child for all eternity.
Amen.

Thérèse and the Eucharist

How sweet was that first kiss of Jesus!
It was a kiss of love.
I felt I was loved and said
'I love you and give myself to you forever!'
There were no demands made, no struggles,
no sacrifices; for a long time now
Jesus and Thérèse looked at
and understood each other.
That day it was not simply a look,
it was a fusion; there were no longer two.
Thérèse had vanished like a drop of water
lost in the immensity of the ocean.
Jesus alone remained.

Thérèse – First Communion

St Thérèse's cousin, Marie Guérin, was so troubled by scruples that she was afraid to receive Holy Communion. Thérèse wrote to her and encouraged her not to pay any attention to these doubts and anxieties: 'Do you not realise', she said to her, 'that Jesus is there in the tabernacle just for you – for you alone? He longs to come into your heart – receive him often, very often. This is the remedy, if you really want to be cured.'

Although Thérèse was only sixteen when she wrote the letter, her words show a deep understanding and appreciation of the Eucharist. At a time when so many of the great spiritual writers of the day were cautiously debating the wisdom of frequent communion, Thérèse reveals a clear insight into the things of God and the mysteries of his love.

As soon as she became aware of what Holy Communion meant, there was nothing she longed for more ardently. When she was only seven years old her sister Céline started her preparation for her First Communion. Thérèse asked to be allowed to attend the instructions, saying that four years was not too long to prepare to receive our Lord.

Her First Communion was, in fact, a turning-point in her life. It was a day of unclouded joy, a real personal meeting between Jesus and herself. How simply and beautifully she herself describes it: 'I knew I was loved and I told him I loved him… something had melted away. Thérèse had disappeared like a drop in the ocean. Tears of happiness flowed as 'all the joy of heaven came flooding into a human heart'.

> Come, Lord, dwell in me.
> Your beauty wins my heart.
> Change me into yourself.

But not all St Thérèse's Communions were like that. How different was her experience in later years! 'Indeed', she wrote, 'I do not know any moment when I experience less consolation than after Communion.' She is forced to admit that she is often overcome by drowsiness and sleep: 'What excuse have I, after all these years in religion, for going through my thanksgiving as if I were asleep?' In fact, she often resolved to prolong her thanksgiving during the day to make up for her poor attempt in the morning.

> Here in the tiny host
> I find the fruit of love.

When Thérèse went to Communion she was more concerned with pleasing our Lord that with pleasing herself. 'After all', she says, 'I am the hostess, so I must not be concerned with my own satisfaction but with his.' She understood so well Jesus' longing to give himself in the Eucharist. 'It is not to remain in a golden ciborium that he comes down from heaven but to find another heaven – the heaven of our souls, in which he takes delight.' Thérèse did not go to Communion to receive merit or reward or to obtain gifts from God. She went because she loved. All she wanted was to please him and to offer him a heart he could truly call his own.

For this reason feelings of unworthiness could never keep Thérèse from Communion. The whole message of her Little Way was one of acceptance of herself as she actually was. Faults, failings and limitations only increased her confidence and her trust in God. 'The Guest of our souls knows our needs; he comes only to find an empty heart – that is all he asks.'

> *It seems to me that when Jesus descends into my heart he is content to find himself so well received and I too am content.*

One day a novice came to Thérèse and told her that because of some fault she was going to stay away from Communion. Thérèse could not agree. 'Instead of closing your heart like that', she said, 'you should open it all the more – then the Bread of Life will nourish you and give you all you need.'

From Her Writings

My Heaven

My heaven lies
within the tiny host,
for, in his love,
my Spouse lies hidden there,
the source divine
from which I draw my life.
There, night and day,
He listens to my prayer.

Poem no. 32. Translation by Santa Clara

I cannot receive Holy Communion as often as I desire, but, Lord, you are all-powerful: remain in me as in a tabernacle.

O living Bread of Heaven
O sacrament most dear,
O mystery of love –
love only can repay.
Come live within my heart.
Jesus the Host's white splendour,
if only for today.

Poem no. 5. Translation by Santa Clara

His presence makes me a living monstrance by his power.

Blest Eucharist,
great mystery of love!
Come in the white host
to my heart and stay,
O Jesus, Bread of heaven,
Bread of life,
Today, only today.

Poem no. 5. Translation by Santa Clara

Petition Prayer

Lord Jesus, through the life of St Thérèse,
you have brought new hope to all
who long to open their hearts to you.
Teach us the secret of her Little Way
and help us to realise that we can
always talk with you and bring you
our gratitude, our smiles and our tears.

Stay with us, Jesus, so that
in the midst of our busy hours,
we may turn to you in loving trust.
Transform each passing moment of time
into a moment of prayer.
Fill every troubled heart with
the confident faith of St Thérèse.
In joy and in sorrow,
in every circumstance,
may our hearts rest in your peace.
Amen.

Thérèse and the Missions

I feel the call to be an Apostle. I would like to travel all over the world, making your name known and planting your cross on heathen soil; only I would not be content with one particular mission, I would want to preach the Gospel on all five continents and in the most distant lands, all at once. And even then it would not do, carrying on my mission for a limited number of years; I would want to have been a missionary from the beginning of creation, and go on being a missionary till the world came to an end.

Less than three years after her canonisation, St Thérèse was proclaimed Patroness of the Missions, quite an extraordinary achievement for someone who never set foot on a mission field and who, during her short life, knew only a few missionaries, mostly by correspondence. If we ask the secret of her immense influence on the missions we find the answer in her own words: 'It is by prayer and sacrifice alone that we as Carmelites can be useful to the Church.'

She herself records the moment when she first realised her call to dedicate her life to the apostolate of prayer. One Sunday, as she was closing her missal, a picture of the Crucifixion slipped from between the pages. A strange emotion swept over her as she realised that Christ's sacrifice is rejected and forgotten by so many. 'My heart was pierced with sorrow', she said, 'to see the precious blood falling, with no one bothering to catch it, and I made up my mind, there and then, to stay in spirit at the foot of the cross, to gather up the dew of heavenly life and give it to others.

From that moment the cry of the dying Saviour, 'I thirst', echoed in my heart and I longed to satisfy his thirst for souls.'

It is for us by prayer to train workers who will spread the good news of the Gospel and save many souls.

Thérèse's decision to give herself to the apostolate of prayer within the walls of the cloistered convent was a deliberate one. During her journey to Rome, someone gave her a copy of the *Missionary Annals* to read. However, she quickly passed them on to her sister Céline, saying: 'I will not read them, for I find I am too anxious for active works, and I wish instead to live a life hidden within the cloisters, so as to give myself more completely to God.' She entered the convent fully aware that her vocation was not to the mission fields as such, but the apostolate of prayer and sacrifice: 'After all', she wrote, 'is not the apostolate of prayer higher that that of the spoken word'?

At one stage of her religious life it was thought that Thérèse might be sent to the new foundation in Hanoi from the Mission Carmel in Saigon, founded from Lisieux in 1861. Instead, however, she was given a joy of a different kind. She was asked to be 'spiritual sister' to two young seminarians, Maurice Bellière and Adolphe Roulland, both preparing to go on the missions. It was a fulfilment of her deepest desire – two young brothers of her own age, future priests and missionaries: 'Not for years had I experienced such happiness', she wrote. 'I felt my soul renewed as if someone had struck a musical string long forgotten.'

The letters she wrote to both of these missionaries contain some of her deepest spiritual insights into the missionary nature of the Church, as well as revealing the warmth of her personal concern for each of them: 'You will only know in heaven', she wrote to Maurice Bellière, 'how dear you are to me. I feel our souls were made to understand each other.'

Through our small acts of charity, hidden and unknown, we obtain the conversion of souls and help many missionaries.

Thérèse's understanding of the missions was clear and focused. She was not concerned with the great missionary questions of the day. Her missionary thrust came from her burning love for God and her intense desire to make him known and loved. 'I shall be truly happy to work with you for the salvation of the souls', she told Father Roulland. 'This is why I became a Carmelite nun, to be a missionary through love.'

Undoubtedly prayers and sacrifices are the best assistance we can give to missionaries.

During her last illness the infirmarian suggested that she take a short walk in the garden each day. One of the sisters noticed how much effort this cost her and advised her to rest. 'It is true', Thérèse replied, 'it is an effort, but do you know what gives me strength? I offer each step for some missionary, thinking that somewhere far away, one of them is worn out from his labours and, to lessen his fatigue, I offer mine to God.'

From Her Writings

To evangelise the evangelists – that is the chief object of all my prayers.

What a mystery indeed! The Creator of the universe awaits my prayer to save a multitude of souls.

How could I ever cease to pray for all missionaries everywhere?

Prayer of St Thérèse for Fr Bellière

Jesus, I thank you for fulfilling one of my greatest wishes, that of having a brother, a priest, an apostle. I feel unworthy of this grace, yet since you have given it to me, I offer for him with joy all my prayers and sacrifices.

You know my one and only ambition is to make you known and loved. My brother will fight on the plain and I, on the mountain of Carmel, will ask you to give him the victory.

Guard him in the midst of dangers, keep his heart for you alone. May he be an apostle worthy of your Sacred Heart.

Mary, Mother of Carmel, I confide him to your care. Teach him to love Jesus as you yourself loved him.

This is my vocation – to be an apostle of apostles.

I do not ask for riches or glory.
I ask for love.
Great deeds are forbidden me,
I can neither preach the gospel
nor shed my blood,
but what does it matter?
Others labour in my stead
and I stay close to Jesus
and love him for all those in the strife.

Prayer for Missionaries

St Thérèse of the Child Jesus,
Patroness of the Missions,
remember your burning desire
while on earth 'to plant the cross of Jesus
in every land and to announce the Gospel
till the end of the time'.
We ask you now to help missionaries everywhere
and inspire them with your love.
Obtain for us an increase of missionary zeal
and generosity.
Protect all who preach the gospel,
support them in their trials and
teach them to love Jesus as you loved him.
Amen.

The Science of Love

Charity was the key to my vocation. The Church must have a heart, a heart burning with love; it is love that imparts life to all its members. I realised that love included every vocation, that love is in all things, that love is eternal, reaching down through the ages and stretching to the utmost limits of the earth.

Beside myself with joy, I cried out: 'Jesus my love, my vocation at last I have found it, my vocation is love'. I have found my place in the Church, and this place, Jesus, you have given me yourself; in the heart of the Church, my Mother, I will be love.

One evening at the end of prayer, St Thérèse read a short sentence from the life of St Margaret Mary that made a deep impression on her. It was a phrase spoken by Our Lord to the saint: 'If you want a guide to dictate all your actions then read the Book of Life, which contains the whole science of loving'.

Thérèse's whole life was a search for the science of love. 'It's the only science I want', she wrote to her sister Marie, 'and I'd barter everything I possess to win it, for it is only love that makes us what God wants us to be'.

> *Jesus, your love is an ocean*
> *that has no shore to bound it.*

For Thérèse, love was not a theory or doctrine: it was a Person. When she died, the nuns were surprised to find carved into the doorpost of her cell the words, 'Jesus, my only love'. Yet from her earliest years she had only one desire, 'to love Jesus and make him loved'. Once she understood God's personal and unique love for her, her response was total and unreserved; she kept nothing back: 'I wish to love Jesus passionately', she wrote, 'and show him a thousand tokens of my love'. The words of Jesus on the cross, 'I thirst', had a special meaning for her. She understood that God not only gives himself in love but seeks our love in return; he is, in her words, 'a beggar in love'.

Thérèse's whole life was a love song; the inexhaustible subject of all her thoughts and of her writings was the love of Jesus, her Friend and Spouse, a focused, burning love that was total and unconditional. Her greatness was not that she discovered the reality of this love but that she lived it at white heat. There is no other way to explain the heroic quality of her life – her daily faithfulness, her unselfish giving, her immense apostolic desires, her joy in suffering and her gentle surrender to her own painful death. Her last words, 'My God, I love you', give meaning to her whole life and to every particular detail of it.

> *My God, you know the only thing*
> *I ever wanted is to love you,*
> *I have no ambition for any other glory except that.*

But Thérèse knew that 'love can only be repaid by love' and that love of itself cannot be hidden or inactive. It does not have to show itself in great deeds or heroic actions; it is, she says, as simple as 'scattering flowers': 'never to miss a single opportunity of making some small sacrifice, here by a smiling look, there by a kindly word; making profit of the very smallest actions and doing it for love'. Thérèse did not have to think up artificial penances; she let providence provide and she was not disappointed. The daily routine of Carmel was enough; the day's assignments carried out, by the hour and by the minute, with honesty and faithfulness, left little room for self-indulgence. For Thérèse love and penance flowed in the same current and she accepted the challenges of community life with open arms. But, once again, she knew the source of this love: 'it is Jesus alone who is acting in me, the more I am united with him, the greater my love for all my sisters without distinction'.

During her last illness, Thérèse saw through the window the setting sun casting its rays over nature and the tops of the trees appeared all golden. 'What a difference', I said to myself, 'if one stays in the shade or on the contrary opens oneself to the sun of love'. She herself, as she testifies in one of her later poems, 'always walked in Love's enchanting flame.'

> *I have flames within me,*
> *I want to be set on fire with love.*

When she was asked if she looked forward to heaven in order to enjoy God she replied, 'No, it is not that which attracts me – it is love; to love, to be loved and to return to earth to make Love loved'. Is it any wonder that her sister Pauline, her 'ideal from childhood and her second mother', wanted to call the first edition of the Autobiography 'A Canticle of Love'.

From Her Writings

O Love now inflame me,
pierce deep as I name thee,
O come, for I claim thee,
consumed may I be!

Poem no.28. Translated by Santa Clara

It seems to me that love possesses and surrounds me, that at each moment this love is renewing me, purifying my soul and not leaving there any trace of sin.

It is natural to love to sacrifice everything, to give in all directions, up and down, back and forth, to squander itself, never calculating, destroying the hope of fruit by plucking the blossoms.

Love gives everything, but we, alas, we give only after reckoning: we hesitate to sacrifice what is advantageous to ourselves. This is not love, for love is blind; it is a wild torrent that leaves nothing behind in the path where it has gone.

Your love has gone before me;
it has grown with me,
and now it is an abyss
whose depths I cannot fathom.

There is no more to say;
everything is accomplished.
Love is the only thing that matters.

Prayer of Intercession

Most loving Father,
you were pleased to give
St Thérèse of the Child Jesus
a trusting spirit of childhood
and surrender to your will
in every circumstance of life:
help us to follow in the path
of simplicity she traced for us.
May we go forward in peace,
accepting the challenge of life
with courage, and walking
faithfully along that way of the Gospel.
Help us to realise that we too
are called to live a life of love
to the glory of your name
and the spread of your kingdom.

Prayer of St Thérèse to obtain Love

Merciful father, in the name of Jesus,
the Virgin Mary and all the saints,
I beg you to enkindle me
with your Spirit of Love
and grant me the favour
of making you greatly loved.

The Hidden Face

Prayer of St Thérèse to the Holy Face

Jesus, in your bitter Passion,
you became a 'Man of Sorrows'.
I venerate your Holy Face,
on which shone the beauty
and gentleness of your Divinity.
In your face, hidden and despised,
I recognise your infinite love,
and I long to love you in return
and make you greatly loved.
One day may I see your glorious Face
in the kingdom of your love.

Pauline, St Thérèse's sister, testified at the beatification process: 'Devotion to the Holy Face was Sr Thérèse's special attraction. As tender as was her devotion to the Child Jesus, it cannot be compared to her devotion to the Holy Face.' As a child, Thérèse was a member of the Confraternity of the Holy Face, but it was not until she entered the convent that the devotion took on particular significance for her: 'Until my entry into Carmel I never fathomed the treasure hidden in the Holy Face'. By the time of her clothing in 1889 it had taken on such importance for her that she obtained permission to change her name to 'Sr Thérèse of the Child Jesus and the Holy Face.'

It was through her meditation on the words of the prophet Isaiah that she entered deeply into the mystery of love hidden and revealed in this devotion: 'There is no beauty in him, no comeliness, we have seen him and there was nothing to attract our eyes.' On her deathbed, Thérèse admitted that 'these words of Isaiah have been the whole foundation of my devotion to the Holy Face.' It was indeed, her sister Céline adds, 'the burning inspiration of her life'. As she meditated on the face of her Beloved, she understood more deeply than ever the value of redemptive suffering; suffering, freely accepted and offered back to God in love, is transformed into grace and glory. Jesus, the suffering Servant, accepts all, gives all, for the salvation of the world: 'to love is to give everything, it is to give oneself'.

Hide me in Thy Face, sweet Lord;
give me Thy love, if only for today.

At the same time the words of Isaiah took on a personal significance for her and gave meaning to the terrible trial of her father's illness, who, a month after Thérèse received the habit, was confined to a mental hospital in Caen. Her father, who had always been the image of her heavenly Father, now became the image of the Son, humiliated and in pain: 'Just as the adorable face of Jesus was veiled during his Passion, so the face of his faithful servant was veiled in the days of his suffering'. Thérèse found her way through her sharing in the suffering of Christ, to the mystery of the cross, the mystery of love. Her longing to share in the passion of Christ sprang from a lover's heart, anxious to unite herself as closely as possible to her Beloved. 'To live for love', she said, 'is to climb Calvary with Jesus'. The Face of Christ was for her the icon of all suffering and redemptive love; the power of transforming grace set free upon the earth.

I feel we must all go to heaven
by the same road –
suffering joined with love.

It is in this context that we must understand Thérèse's longing to be hidden and forgotten. Behind the veil of the ordinary and the commonplace, she could live out her life quietly and unnoticed. How well she achieved her aim is clear from the telling remark of one of the sisters: 'Why, we don't even see her practising virtue!' Status or approval did not concern her, for she knew whom she was following: 'O Face that was not recognised even by your own disciples'.

Yet when she died and the sisters were asked to give their abiding memory of her, it was without doubt what they called the 'angel's eye': her wondrous, beautiful and unforgettable smile, a smile that hid her own suffering and lightened that of others. 'I try, with God's grace, never to burden others with the trials God sees fit to send me'. The convent chaplain called her a 'singing soul' and the Prioress described her as 'one whose head is filled with tricks – she can make you shed tears one minute or split your sides with laughing the next'. It was the human face of Christ Thérèse admired, as much in his joy and compassion as in his pain and suffering.

One of the last photographs of Thérèse shows her holding two pictures which symbolised her name and her vocation, one of the Child Jesus, the other of the Holy Face. All her desires had been fulfilled; the child had become the woman, the woman the saint and the saint transformed into her Beloved.

> *Look into the Face of Jesus,*
> *there you will see*
> *how much he loves you.*

FROM HER WRITINGS

*O! how much good
the picture of the Holy Face
has done me in my life.*

*The petals of my flowers
caress Thy Sacred Face,
They tell me that my heart
has fled to thee above,
Thou knowest well the language
my leaf-strewn roses trace,
and thou art smiling at my love.*

Poem no. 34. Translated by Santa Clara

*Life is often burdensome.
Yes, life is an effort,
it is hard to begin a day's work.
If only we could be aware of Jesus
but no, he seems
a thousand miles away.*

*I beg you, Father, look upon me
only in the Face of Jesus and
in his heart, burning with love.*

Make my soul a sanctuary.
Thy holy dwelling place;
Make it a garden of delight
Where every flower sees the Light:
The glory of Thy Face.

Translated by Ronald Knox

Prayer to St Thérèse

St Thérèse of the Child Jesus
and the Holy Face,
teach us to follow your way
of confidence and trust.
Help us to realise that
a father's love watches over us
each day of our lives.
Obtain for us the light to see,
in sorrow as in joy,
in trials as in peace,
the loving hand of our Father.
Give us your own faith and trust,
so that we may walk in darkness,
as in the light, holding fast
to the way of love,
knowing as you did,
that everything is a grace.

Jesus, Thine image, fair to trace,
shall be my star, where'er I go,
Thou knowest, in Thy sacred face,
I find my heaven, while here below.

My only treasure is Thy face,
no other do I see,
there shall I find my hiding-place
till, Jesus, I resemble Thee.

Poem no. 20. Translated by Santa Clara

The Death of a Saint

I feel that my mission is soon to begin, my mission to make God loved as I love him, to teach others my Little Way.

If God grants my desires, my heaven will be spent on earth until the end of time. Yes, I want to spend my heaven doing good on earth.

I can't rest as long as there are souls to be saved. But when the angel says: 'Time is no more!' then I will take my rest.

I will be able to rejoice because the number of the elect will be complete, and all will have entered into joy and repose. My heart beats with joy at this thought.

Two years before she died, St Thérèse wrote to her aunt: 'I love reading the lives of the saints and I have sometimes envied the happy lot of those who lived in their company and enjoyed their holy conversations.' Without realising it, she was describing her own story, but with the roles reversed; as she was dying it was her sisters who had the privilege of looking after a saint and listening to her last conversations.

On Good Friday 1896, Thérèse coughed blood, the first sign of the consumption that eventually led to her death. She herself thought death would come quickly but the slow and painful process of dying was to last eighteen months. At first she made little of her illness but, as her strength failed, she had to acknowledge its presence more and more and in July 1897 she was transferred to the infirmary. While she was there her sister Pauline visited her each day and began to record the conversations she had with her. She seemed to have some intuition of Thérèse's future mission. Whatever the reason, the seven hundred random notes, scribbled on pieces of paper, have given to the world a most extraordinary spiritual treasure, known in English as the *Last Conversations*. In it we see the real Thérèse, a saint with a human face, weak and vulnerable, struggling with darkness and with pain; once and for all, the statue is stripped bare and the stereotype image destroyed.

> *If some of the saints were to return to earth*
> *I wonder how many of them would recognise*
> *themselves in what has been written about them.*

In *The Story of a Soul*, Thérèse gives a glimpse into the life of a saint; in the *Last Conversations*, on the other hand, often with frightening realism, we enter into the death of a saint. It is very different from what we might expect; we watch a saint die, inch by inch, with every sigh and convulsion preserved with stark clarity, as if under a microscope. There was nothing glamorous about her dying. She was not spared the natural torments of burning fever, excruciating thirst, and the relentless coughing: 'I cough and cough', she said, 'like and old train coming into a station.' Her whole body was racked with extreme weakness, powerlessness and distress: 'Last night I couldn't take any more – never would I have believed I could suffer so much.'

Added to her physical torment was a terrible crisis of faith, that lasted until the moment of her death – she lost all sense of God's presence and heaven seemed nothing but a dream and mirage. She searched for images to express the reality: 'a thick fog, a darkened tunnel, a wall stretching up to heaven'. The arguments of the worst rationalists filled her mind and she was plagued with the mocking spirits of unbelief. 'The darkness itself seems to mock me; death will not give what you long for, but rather a greater darkness still and a night of non-existence'.

> *Our Lord died on the cross in agony,*
> *and yet this was the most*
> *beautiful death of love.*

Yet in suffering and in the face of death her deepest self is revealed: 'I can explain my suffering only by my ardent desire to save souls.' Thérèse's Little Way faced the ultimate challenge, the personal encounter with pain, suffering and desolation and did not fail. 'How consoled I am to know that my agony resembles that of my Saviour.' Her death becomes the testament of her life and the ultimate triumph of the Little Way.

A few hours before she died, Thérèse gave this testament, sealed with her own life's experience: 'I have never sought anything but the truth.' It was this truth that made her free, free to be a mighty instrument in the hand of God, a universal sister to a searching world and a saint as ageless as the Gospel itself. In the end her life, her death and her message were one.

> *I am not dying*
> *I am entering into life.*

When she died on the evening of 30 September in the presence of her community, the Prioress turned to her sisters and said 'Open all the doors'. 'It seemed to me', her sister Pauline remarked, 'that at that moment, the same command rang throughout heaven.' And today, one hundred years later, it seems to many people that, because of Thérèse, those doors have never been fully closed.

From Her Writings

If I did not suffer from one minute to the next, it would be impossible for me to be patient. I do not look further than the present moment. It is when we think too much of the past or the future that we become discouraged and lose hope.

I see what I have believed. I possess what I have hoped for. I am united to the one I have loved with all the strength of my loving.

Living by Love

To live by love is not to rest
on Tabor's blissful height;
There is another hill I know,
More precious in my sight;
Love follows the Beloved still
To Calvary again,
To share with him the mystery
Of loneliness and pain.

Poem no. 17. Translated by R. Knox

Do not be sad at seeing me so ill: see how happy God makes me! As regards dying, I feel only joy: what joy to see him and to be judged by him whom in life we have loved so much.

How easy it it to become
discouraged when you are sick.

'Of St Thérèse of Lisieux it can be said with conviction that God chose her to reveal directly to the men and women of our own time the central reality of the Gospel, that God is our Father and we are his children. This is the unique genius of St Thérèse of Lisieux. Thanks to her the entire Church has found once again the whole simplicity and freshness of this Gospel truth, which has its origin and source in the heart of Christ himself.

John Paul II – Lisieux 1980

God, our Father, you promised your kingdom to these who are willing to become like little children. Help us to follow the way of St Thérèse with confidence, so that by her prayers we may come to know your eternal glory.

Mass of St Thérèse

Doctor of the Church

On 19 October 1997 – Mission Sunday – Pope John Paul II declared St Thérèse of Lisieux a doctor of the Church in Rome. It is indeed ironic that someone whose deepest desire in life was to remain 'hidden, unknown and forgotten' should have yet another title and status conferred on her, this time in the centenary year of her death. She now finds herself in the company of those whom she herself referred to in her autobiography as 'holy doctors who illuminate the Church with the clarity of their teaching'.

A doctor in the making
The idea of a doctorate for Thérèse was not new. In fact it was first seriously proposed over sixty years ago during an International Congress to mark the solemn blessing of the Crypt in the new Basilica in Lisieux in 1932. A French Jesuit, Gustave Debuquois, prepared a substantial dossier outlining the various arguments in favour of such a declaration. His proposal caused quite a stir and a lot of public debate. Things moved quickly and gathered momentum until it was officially silenced with a resounding salvo from Rome: *obstat sexus*: Thérèse was a woman!

It was not until 1970 that the obstacle was removed. In August of that year Paul VI declared Teresa of Avila a doctor of the Church and one week later added the name of Catherine of Siena to the list. It was the first time in the history of the Church that such a declaration had been made. Until that time, of the thirty doctors of the Church, none were women – all were either bishops, priests or deacons.

Doctor of the Church is a title given to Christian writers whose teaching has significantly enriched and enlivened the doctrine of the Church. The conditions generally required for such a declaration include: great sanctity, eminent learning and a doctrine of universal appeal and importance to the whole Church. Of Thérèse's sanctity there is no question; she has been universally acclaimed as the 'greatest saint of modern times', and now her new and creative restatement of the central message of the Christian faith has received added importance with this official declaration.

A saint with a backbone
The title of doctor will add nothing to Thérèse herself. It will hardly lessen her popularity, as some fear, for she is already deeply embedded in the devotional life of the Church. She is the people's saint, 'the worker's saint' Dorothy Day called her, to express how much ordinary people have identified with her; behind the veil, the cloister and the grille, they saw her as one of themselves, one who had sanctified the ordinary, the humdrum and the everyday. There is a wholesomeness about her approach to life and a sense of reality that makes people comfortable with her. She expressed herself with great clarity and simplicity at the level where ordinary people need to be touched and be healed. Her own sister Pauline once referred to her as a 'saint with a backbone'.

But a doctorate is not about popularity. It is not even about influence or orthodoxy; Thérèse's doctrine was already fully approved by her canonisation. It is about significance and meaning: ecclesiastical significance and universal meaning. It is about mission. The question is, in what way is Thérèse of Lisieux a teacher, not just for her own time and culture, but for the Universal Church of every age? Does her wisdom and her understanding of the Gospel profoundly transform our understanding of the Christian message? Is her experience 'cosmic', in the sense that it will enrich the minds and hearts of those still searching for God in the third millennium and does she offer a key that transcends and transforms the historical confines of our age as well as her own?

A theologian with a difference

St Thérèse of Lisieux is one of the great theologians of this century. But she is a theologian with a difference. Her writings do not form a systematic or dogmatic synthesis of the Christian life. Rather she is a theologian of experience, a narrative theologian, whose doctrine is contained within her story, in much the same way as the teaching of Jesus is contained within the Gospel narrative. It is impossible to separate the theology of Thérèse from her story; all her writings are autobiographical and her experiences, upon which she reflected so deeply, were all grace-filled reflections of life. For her 'everything is a grace'.

Thérèse is a young theologian, young in mind and young at heart. It is not without significance that the first announcement of her being declared a doctor of the Church was made at an international gathering of young people in Paris. She never grew old, except in wisdom and grace. She vibrates with joy and enthusiasm; she never lost her dream of youth or her vision of what might be. 'From the youth of St Thérèse', John Paul II has written, 'spring forth her enthusiasm for the Lord, the intensity of her love and her realistic daring. The charm of her holiness is confirmation that God grants in abundance, even to the young, the treasures of his wisdom.'

A woman's heart

And she is a woman; a feminine theologian, who speaks with a woman's heart and whose mode of expression is distinctly feminine. Central to the whole rediscovery of feminine theology today is the fact that there is a distinctive vision that goes with the feminine way of looking at life. Thérèse certainly wrote from a woman's perspective. She trusted her own experiences and her own insights and was not afraid to express them and defend them. She was in touch with her own vulnerability and her own weakness and at the same time open to the divine fire and overpowering tenderness and gentleness of God. Her teaching and her doctrine have given to a world permeated with fear and rigorism, a fresh and original understanding of the Christian message. The doctorate of St Thérèse is a welcome antidote to a male, rational expression of the Gospel and a timely challenge to a Church that has for so long ignored its own feminine roots.

My only love

Nowhere do we see the whole theological focus of Thérèse so clearly as in her understanding of the Incarnation. The primacy of charity and the centrality of Christ find expression in almost every document of Vatican II. With good reason Thérèse has been called 'the saint of the Council', its prophet and forerunner. Her theology was totally incarnational, her love for Jesus immediate and passionate. For Thérèse the primacy of love was, above all, a personal, focused love of her Spouse and Saviour. 'Jesus, my only love', were words she carved, not only on the doorpost of her cell, but carried in her heart, day and night. We have only to read the burning words of love found in Manuscript B – 'an echo of the heart of God', her sister called them – her later poems or some of the letters to her sister Céline, to discover how passionately she was consumed with love for 'Jesus, my only friend'. For Thérèse, Jesus himself is the 'Doctor of Doctors who teaches without the sound of words'. It is not enough to call Thérèse a doctor of love, as she has already been named. She is a doctor of the love of Jesus and her life was a love-song and a celebration of that love.

A child of the Church

In his classic study of St Thérèse, Hans Urs Von Balthasar

claims that the Church is in constant need of a 'blood transfusion from the lives of the saints'. The Church is shaped as much by the lives of its saints as by its teaching or its doctrine. They inject new life into failing structures, challenging set ideas and ageing formulas. They are the real revolutionaries who love the Church so much they will not leave her alone. In her autobiography, *The Story of a Soul*, Thérèse refers to herself a number of times as a 'child of the Church'; the Church was her mother, and it was within its burning heart that she found her place and her vocation. Thérèse was not trying to change or even challenge the Church by her writings or her teaching; her place was within the Church, touching it at its very centre, like a mother bringing forth her children in pain and suffering. If Thérèse's doctorate means anything for a fragile Church in a post-modern world it is surely a call to acknowledge its own brokenness and sinfulness; a Church needing forgiveness and pardon for itself, as well as imparting it to others. The doctorate of Thérèse is an invitation to the whole Body of Christ to rediscover its own burning heart and reflect the human face of God to a world waiting for his message of love.

The little doctor

The school chaplain, Abbé Domin, nicknamed Thérèse his 'little doctor'. It is a title she would now happily embrace. Her life is a celebration of littleness. Though the word is so easily misunderstood Thérèse was in fact saying something very important and profound. Most of us live our lives in the ordinary, humdrum events of the everyday. For Thérèse this is where the greatness lies; small is important, small is powerful, small is beautiful. It is the Gospel concept of 'the little ones' who will inherit the kingdom, the *anawim* beloved by God. Thérèse probably never heard of 'the option for the poor', but she would have been delighted with the phrase 'option for the little'. For her, such an option is a call to the very heart of the Gospel and to the freedom of the children of God; a call to respect the uniqueness of every person as a child of God and to listen to the Spirit speaking in the heart of the people. 'This is the message of Thérèse that we are called to shout aloud today', John Paul II exclaims, '*each one is loved by God* '. It is the duty of the Church to proclaim this message to the whole of humanity'.

At its very core this is what the doctorate of St Thérèse of Lisieux is all about: the proclamation of the Gospel.

The impossible dream

A young girl plays on the sand
no one knows her name;
A young woman cloistered in light
no one sees her face;
a nun young and frail in a desert of pain
her story written in blood.
The desert blooms, a flower grows in the sand.
High above the rocks an eagle soars
a fledgling nestled in its wing.
Love explodes and falls like crystals
on the ground; fear has no hiding-place.
Love is a terrible thing, a wild torrent
flooding a boundless shore
to die before it lives.
I heard an echo from the heart of God,
a cry – a beggar's cry: I thirst.
He came – the shy one – like a thief;
a lover's kiss, to spur impossible dreams.
Passion, fire, holocaust, here consume.
The naked rose is spent.
All is grace.

Eugene McCaffrey